LOCAL STORY

Kristen Palmer

BROADWAY PLAY PUBLISHING INC
New York
www.broadwayplaypublishing.com
info@broadwayplaypublishing.com

LOCAL STORY
© Copyright 2019 Kristen Palmer

Cover art by Kelly Campbell

First edition: March 2019
I S B N: 978-0-88145-824-4

Book design: Marie Donovan
Page make-up: Adobe InDesign
Typeface: Palatino

LOCAL STORY was presented as a part of the 2nd
Annual Capital Fringe Festival by MadCap Players
(Artistic Director, Christopher Snipe; Managing
Director Shawn Helm) at the Goethe Institute—
Gallery. It opened on 19 July 2007. The cast and
creative contributors were:

JIMMY .... Tyler Smith
BUBBA .... Cliff Williams III
BETSY .... Tori Miller
ROY .... William C Cook
AMORY .... Jewel Greenberg
GLORIA .... Kate Hundely
D'LADY .... Katie Atkinson

Director .... Christopher Snipe
Assistant director .... Hilary Trudell
Stage manager .... Tiffany Ford
Set designer .... Beth Baldwin
Costume designer .... Elizabeth D Reeves
Lighting designer .... Brian S Allard
Sound designer .... Matthew Bruce

LOCAL STORY was produced by Karen Smith, Phillip C Curry, Inger Tudor, and Michelle Hilyard in association with Theater of NOTE at Theater of NOTE in Los Angeles. It opened 29 November 2007. The cast and creative contributors were:

D'LADY	Michelle Hilyard
BUBBA	David Wilcox
JIMMY	Jeffrey Emerson
BETSY	Mandi Moss
ROY	Monroe Makowsky
AMORY	Jennifer Anne Evans
GLORIA	Elizabeth Liang
Director	Inger Tudor
Stage manager	Bree Todish
Set designer	Erin Brewster
Lighting designer	Jennifer Dallas
Sound design	Mark McClain Wilson
Costume consultant	Joel Scher

LOCAL STORY was produced by Overlap Productions (Artistic Directors Susanna L Harris & Tania Inessa Kirkman) at Access Theater in NYC. It opened 28 November 2007. The cast and creative contributors were:

D'LADY .... Sarah Kate Jackson
BUBBA .... Travis York
JIMMY .... Mark David Watson
BETSY .... Keira Keeley
GLORIA .... Marielle Heller
AMORY .... Havilah Brewster
ROY .... Ben Scaccia

Director .... Susanna L Harris
Stage manager .... Susan Sunday
Sets .... Kina Park
Lighting .... Ben Kato
Sound .... Amy Altadonna
Costumes .... Jessica Gaffney

SPECIAL THANKS

Everyone involved in readings, workshops and productions in living rooms and theaters in Seattle, DC, Philadelphia, NYC and Charlotte, SC from early scenes in 1999 to publication in 2019. New Georges, The Flea, Blue Coyote Theater Group, Printers Devil Theatre, NascentWorks,Theater of NOTE, Cardboard Box Collective, Indie Theater Now, and the Creative Arts Team. Tim Farrell, Gary Winter, Heidi Schreck, Michael Gladis, Travis York, Flora Diaz, Mariana Newhard, Jim Ireland, Meg MacCary, LaVonda Elam, Dumeha Vernice Thompson, Christopher Burris, Chime Day Serra, Deron Bos, Kip Fagan, Paul Willis, Jen Kays, David Vegh, Stephen Hando, Andrew Beal, Matt Ford, Jessica Pregnolato, Martin Denton, Rochelle Denton, Tina Kunz, Alyssa Ford, Susan Louise O'Connor, and other actors and artists who shared their voices and their thoughts with me while writing this play. Fred Franklin, James Zitz, Amanda Revere, Adam Szymkowicz, Betty & David Michel, John & Rhoda Szymkowicz. This play began when I began writing plays, I'm sure I'm missing really important people from this list, please accept my thanks.

CHARACTERS & SETTING

JIMMY, *a boy, 28*
BUBBA, *a guy, 29*
BETSY, *a girl from Colorado, 24*
ROY, *a husband, 32*
AMORY, *a wife, 34*
GLORIA, *a woman, 30*
D'LADY, *28*

The play takes place in August, in the present day, in a small town in the upper south/mid-west of America.

STAGING NOTES

Scenes should follow quickly on each other, ideally with no scene changes necessary.

for Adam

1.

(BUBBA *and* JIMMY'*s house*)

(*A battered easy chair and a phone on the floor in a dim yellowy light. A mess of colored wires and mechanical parts next to and in front of the chair. Three stacks of books, papers and pamphlets are scattered on the floor and a low, dark brown, shellacked pasteboard table, some are also in the chair. A wall behind the chair with layers of wall covering— paint and wall paper—a darker place where a picture used to be. Newspaper clippings and hand written pages are taped on the wall.*)

(*The phone has been ringing a very long time.*)

(BUBBA *lays inert on the floor next the phone. He is wearing one orange sock, a white T-shirt and boxers.*)

(JIMMY *enters through a screen door. The door continues to flap on its hinges as he passes through it, his arms full of groceries and books.*)

(*Lights brighten slightly.*)

JIMMY: Bubba? Hey man—you going to answer that?

(JIMMY *nudges* BUBBA *with his foot.* BUBBA *doesn't move.*)

JIMMY: Bubba? Dammit. C'mon man. (*He struggles to put down his bags and answer the phone.*) Hello?

BUBBA: (*Not moving*) Is it D'Lady?

JIMMY: (*Over-lapping* BUBBA) Hello? I said Hel-lo? It's nobody. (*He hangs up the phone.*)

BUBBA: She never calls.

JIMMY: That's cause she doesn't love you.

BUBBA: She used to call, then she stopped.

JIMMY: That's cause she used to love you. Then she stopped.

BUBBA: She calls other people.

JIMMY: No, I don't think she does. I don't think anyone's heard from her since she ditched me in Colorado 'bout three years ago.

BUBBA: She must of found someone.

JIMMY: To love?

BUBBA: Maybe. Probably not—probably just some place better.

JIMMY: She comes from crazy.

BUBBA: You seen my other sock?

JIMMY: The red one?

BUBBA: No, the orange—you color blind?

JIMMY: I saw a yellow one outside the bathroom door last week. I would have mentioned it then, but it made me so mad I threw it out the window.

BUBBA: Oh, well. I need the orange one now.

JIMMY: You going out?

BUBBA: No.

JIMMY: You should—there's parties out there, there's people—there's movies and races out there and your sister'd stop calling me.

BUBBA: Just tell her I'm fine.

JIMMY: Right— Well Amory, he doesn't leave the house, he falls asleep in the middle of sentences— But don't worry—he's fine, just fine—he's working on his—his what? What are you working on?

BUBBA: Local history.

JIMMY: Dude—you're passing out half the time—

BUBBA: Don't worry, I figured out a system, once its implemented I'm all set.

JIMMY: What sort of system?

BUBBA: Bells.

(BUBBA connects his device and sets off a godawful racket. JIMMY stares at him until BUBBA turns it off.)

JIMMY: This helps?

BUBBA: It's set to go off at intervals—whenever it goes off I am reminded to pay attention to what I am doing. The bells will keep me on track, focused. You get the books?

JIMMY: Yeah, they didn't have the one on the church—but here's the one on the civil war, and local genealogies.

BUBBA: Check this out—whole thing about a bunch of kids seeing a ghost out by the river. They interview all of them—look at this—murky picture and everything.

JIMMY: Huh, weird.

BUBBA: What about the library—property records from the Sixties? Did they have those?

JIMMY: Couldn't find them. I ran into Roy—said he's coming by later.

BUBBA: I wish you'd've told him I wasn't home.

JIMMY: You're always home. I'm going out.

BUBBA: You looking for somebody?

JIMMY: Nah, not anymore.

BUBBA: Somebody's looking for you.

JIMMY: Nah—

BUBBA: Phone's not ringing for me. What was her name again?

JIMMY: Betsy. Tiny Betsy.

(*Bells go off.* BUBBA *looks at* JIMMY *then gets into his books.* JIMMY *exits. Throws a sock at* BUBBA *from off stage. It is blue.*)

BUBBA: That's not the one I need!

2.

(*The sound of a highway, a warm red desert sunset, heat and dust*)

(BETSY *speaks from a great distance. She is transparent.*)

BETSY: This field is endless. In every direction. It swallows me. Gulp. It swallows me whole. Doesn't even bother to chew.

One year the water stopped. There was a drought and all the melons died. That was when Jimmy was here. Now it's just me. If there were trees I'd watch them change—there are not so I watch the melons grow. I've been growing too. Getting bigger. I think I want to go east. I think I will go east and when I get there, I think I will look for him, till I find him, and when I find him, then I think I'll stop.

(*The sun sets. Night falls deep indigo blue and a starless sky.* BETSY *sticks her thumb out. Holds out a sign that says "Jimmy". Headlights come up bright on her.*)

BETSY: I can see him dreaming. In the morning he's dreaming. In the morning the sun comes up and he dreams he wakes up and sees my head on his pillow. And he thinks in his dream 'if I roll over I will touch her face so gently, so she won't wake up,' and he moves to do this. He rolls over and opens his eyes to look, and when he opens his eyes I am not there. The space is empty, and his fingers send a wish—bring her back—as they rest on his thigh with a sigh and their wish brings me closer.

(Car lights approach. BETSY *looks straight at them.)*

BETSY: There's a knock. He opens the door. It is not me and his belly says, "Betsy"and his mouth says, "hello"and "how're you doing?"and "come in."All the while his belly whispers, "Betsy, her, Betsy"sending out a wish, and I get closer.

(A car stops. A radio playing classic rock is barely audible. Sound of a car door opening. BETSY *gets in. Sound of a car driving off. Crickets)*

3.

*(*ROY *and* AMORY's *house. She is sitting on a tasteful couch, editing a story in her robe and nightgown and sipping herbal tea. She has a lap top computer in front of her, a neat folder of papers, and a* Strunk & White's Manual of Style *within arms reach.)*

*(*ROY *enters, distraught. He is over-dressed for the weather and badly shaven.)*

ROY: Amory! Again! I saw it again—twice now—two times, same place—same time even—corner of my eye—there it is—my pulse racing, hands sweating.

AMORY: Roy, I'm working—

ROY: Sorry—It's just, this keeps happening—this feeling behind me then—

AMORY: People see weird lights all the time—

ROY: It's no light I'm seeing. It's a woman chasing her head around. I should ask your brother, he's studying this stuff right?

AMORY: Ghosts? I think so, though he never mentioned anything about a decapitation—

ROY: No—no—it's not being cut off—it's rolling away from her.

AMORY: Maybe get yourself some tea or something?

ROY: You're very calm about this.

AMORY: I'm not certain that you're seeing what you think you're seeing.

ROY: I did—I saw—

AMORY: Okay, so you saw something. Go ask Bubba. I need to finish this.

ROY: Amory, you are cold.

AMORY: And you're over-excited.

ROY: I know. I know. It's just—it calms me to drive out there—past the bent oak, the fields, the curvy part before the creek bed, the eroding hillside—

AMORY: D'lady's old place?

ROY: Sure, but that's not—

AMORY: And now you're seeing what? Ghosts chasing their heads?

ROY: What do you think it means?

AMORY: You figure it out.

ROY: I don't know—

AMORY: Look. When did you first see it?

ROY: Tuesday, then again tonight, but—

AMORY: She's back—at her mom's. Gloria said she got in Tuesday.

(Lightning. The opening volley of a summer downpour)

(Lights up at BUBBA's house. He sits in his chair, next to a stack of old newspapers. GLORIA stands.)

GLORIA: I just don't want her "dropping by" —I know what that would do to you.

BUBBA: I'm fine—thanks for the papers—I started going through them—

GLORIA: Bubba, listen—I know you know what I mean. You're doing better—you're—busy at something— she's liable to waltz in here, sniffin' around for whatever she needs to make herself feel better for a second and then she'll take off again and you—

BUBBA: I get it Glo.

GLORIA: She hasn't come by my place either.

BUBBA: Well—maybe she's laying low.

GLORIA: Have you called her yet? —You know— anyone let her know that we know she's here?

BUBBA: I burnt up her numbers.

GLORIA: You want to see her though—don't you?

BUBBA: Do you?

GLORIA: It's been what, five years?

BUBBA: Uh huh.

GLORIA: You need a plan. You can't just let her come in and start off with you again like nothing ever happened—she'll try that you know? You've got to be ready. You've got to know exactly what you're going to say—do not let her off the hook.

BUBBA: Maybe she won't even come by.

GLORIA: She will. Bubba—she will. I'm serious—I want you to be okay—don't let her turn you upside down then leave you for me and Jimmy and Amory to deal with—

BUBBA: Glo—I won't. I'm fine anyways. If I see her or not.

GLORIA: You don't have to see her. Someone walks out on you, you owe them nothing. Nothing—not pleasantries, not hospitality—

BUBBA: I'm just not thinking about it. I'm thinking about the way things were before—

GLORIA: Bubba!

BUBBA: Not with her—here—this place—Before those developments went in—

GLORIA: Okay. Well—don't let her hijack this—

BUBBA: Work.

GLORIA: Work you're doing here.

BUBBA: Doubt she'll even notice—wonder what she's doing back anyway?

(BUBBA's *phone rings.* BUBBA *and* GLORIA *jump, startled.*)

(*Lights come up on* AMORY *on the phone at her house.*)

BUBBA: Hello?

AMORY: Bubba. Why aren't you out?

BUBBA: Amory. It's going to rain.

AMORY: Jimmy said he would take you out.

BUBBA: I'm a little busy right now.

AMORY: Doing what? Is D'lady over there?

BUBBA: No. I'm reading—or I was, Glo's over here now.

AMORY: Tell her to call me.

BUBBA: Call Amory.

GLORIA: Tell her I will. Bubba—be careful—

BUBBA: Don't worry. I'm ready as I'm going to be. Don't get caught in the storm. Wait a second. Amory—can I borrow your typewriter?

AMORY: You can have my old one.

BUBBA: Would you—?

GLORIA: Yes. Course I will.

BUBBA: Thanks.

(GLORIA exits.)

AMORY: You know she's here don't you? Gloria told you, right?

BUBBA: Yes. I know. Gloria told me and warned me and prepared me—and I'm fine. Okay? Would you drop it?

AMORY: Alright, just checking. She bring you those old newspapers from her attic?

BUBBA: Yeah—she did. I'm trying to follow a few people—there's this girl—

(Laughter is heard from outside, mixed up with a wind and storm sounds.)

AMORY: You hear something?

BUBBA: Something—the wind probably.

AMORY: Shhhh.

(The laughter gets louder. BUBBA goes to look out the window.)

BUBBA: I don't see anything.

AMORY: Careful. Roy says there're ghosts out there.

(BUBBA shouts out the window.)

BUBBA: Hey! Who's out there? Hello?

(The laughter stops abruptly, only the wind is left.)

BUBBA: Nothing.

(Lightning. Lights out on BUBBA.)

(ROY enters and sits awkwardly next to AMORY. She hangs up the phone. He leans into her, tries to touch her knee.)

ROY: Amory.

AMORY: Shh, the news is coming on.

(ROY *gives* AMORY *a brief kiss on the cheek.*)

(AMORY *cursorily acknowledges it and then gets to work, typing, listening, typing.*)

ROY: She is clean. When we first met, her smell struck me, a continual cleanliness—like a self-cleaning oven. Later I would witness the range and depth of her toiletries and I would stand transfixed in contemplation of the resources invested in the creation of the effect, which was her aura and was what I desired. That she is with me now is a miracle of effort and careful, conscious devotion.
Amory, Amory, I think I would like some coffee maybe, Amory?

AMORY: We don't drink coffee any longer. It makes us nervous.

ROY: Then maybe I'll fix a plate of eggs, some toast— did you get some from the woman down the road?

AMORY: No eggs. The cholesterol, the hormones—no chicken is pure anymore.

ROY: Her's are. She's been selling us eggs for years.

AMORY: Roy. She died. For a while I got them from the supermarket, but then I got thinking about those hens forced into maximum ovulation, never conceiving—

ROY: She died?

AMORY: Yes. Months ago.

ROY: How could I not have noticed? What can I have?

AMORY: Soy crackers, juice and green tea.

ROY: Thank you.

(AMORY *looks up from her work.*)

ROY: For feeding me with intention. ...I'll be in the workshop.

AMORY: No snack?

ROY: No.

AMORY: Roy— Tonight is a good night, you should come to bed when you've settled down a bit.

ROY: Tonight?

AMORY: You can't choose these things.

ROY: I know, but—

AMORY: Just come to bed.

ROY: Yes. In a bit.

(Rain pours onto the roof. Streaming water from the window reflects onto AMORY *as she types and consults her notes.)*

4.

*(*BUBBA *stands in the middle of his room. Staring at* D'LADY *who stands in the doorway winded from running, she's drenched and holding an umbrella.)*

D'LADY: Hi.

BUBBA: You're soaked.

D'LADY: Yeah… It's crazy out there. Pouring—I just went out for a walk—out along the ridge there? You ever go up there?

BUBBA: No.

D'LADY: You should—anyway I even had an umbrella—my mom told me to take an umbrella. I'm staying at my mom's—

BUBBA: I heard.

D'LADY: You didn't call.

BUBBA: Yeah.

D'LADY: Well, I just got here—

BUBBA: Tuesday.

D'LADY: Uh-huh. Took me about a week—I drove.

BUBBA: Course.

D'LADY: Um—it's kinda chilly—

BUBBA: Sorry—you want a towel?

D'LADY: Uh-huh—could I borrow a shirt or something?

BUBBA: Just a minute. *(He exits into the house.)*

(D'LADY starts poking through BUBBA's papers and things.)

D'LADY: I'm glad you were home.
You saved me from drowning nearly.

BUBBA: *(Off-stage)* Yeah. I'm usually here.

D'LADY: Doing what?

BUBBA: *(Off-stage)* For a long time I painted pictures of you on the walls of my mind.

D'LADY: Hah! *(Quietly)* I etched your head in restaurant windows all across the country—

(BUBBA re-enters with towel and a long-sleeved flannel shirt.)

BUBBA: This okay?

D'LADY: Yeah. Thanks. *(She dries off and changes her shirt.)*

BUBBA: Oh, sorry. *(He turns around.)*

D'LADY: What is all this stuff anyway?

BUBBA: Nothing.

D'LADY: Doesn't look like nothing.

BUBBA: I was watching T V a couple years ago. Saw this lady on P B S—it was a program on "how to change your life" or re-claim it—or bring energy? Something. Anyway she said to just start something. The most important thing is to just start something. Start a project—small large doesn't matter. Just do something.

D'LADY: Looks like you did.

BUBBA: I don't know. I started doing research. Documenting. Trying to write it down before it disappears.

D'LADY: Write what down?

BUBBA: Everything—everything that goes on here— kindof like the history—

D'LADY: That's crazy. You can turn around now. Nothing happens here.

BUBBA: It does. People just don't pay attention.

D'LADY: Cause nothing happens.

BUBBA: Things do though. There's plaques all over the place. Plaques about people who came here. Plaques for the dead. There's one—whole story about this girl who disappeared—down by the old dock.

D'LADY: Huh. I went down there yesterday. Why'd they clear all those trees?

BUBBA: Condos. But they had to stop—there was a cemetery.

D'LADY: Really?

BUBBA: Slaves maybe—soldiers? Indians? Some folks from the Smithsonian are coming down—I wrote to see if they needed help but nobody's gotten back to me.

D'LADY: Are they looking for help?

BUBBA: Maybe. I don't know. How about you—what'd you find out there? I heard you were modeling?

D'LADY: A while ago. Not really anything. Mostly waitressing. Bartending—this and that.

BUBBA: Oh. Course. Someone said you got married?

D'LADY: Really? Who to?

BUBBA: Yeah—I didn't believe it. You'd've called if you were, if something big happened to you.

D'LADY: Yeah. Nothing big happened to me. *(She moves to pick up* BUBBA's *papers.)*

BUBBA: Don't—

D'LADY: What?

BUBBA: They're organized.

D'LADY: I just want to look at them—I'm not going to mess them up.

*(*BUBBA *moves in to stop* D'LADY. *In doing so he touches her hand. Everything changes for a moment.)*

BUBBA: D'lady—

D'LADY: Bubba—

*(*BUBBA's *bell system clangs on furiously.)*

D'LADY: Jesus—

BUBBA: Sorry that's just—

D'LADY: What?

BUBBA: My SYSTEM

D'LADY: BUBBA! Turn it off!

BUBBA: I am—here—just—

*(*BUBBA *goes to fix the bells, there is a ridiculous amount of wires and he tries to maintain his conversation with* D'LADY *while getting the thing to shut up.)*

D'LADY: Is this an alarm or something? Are you alarming me?

BUBBA: No—No—it's—it's just to keep me on track—- I fall asleep sometimes?

D'LADY: What do you mean you fall asleep?

BUBBA: Just a minute—I'll get this quiet—

D'LADY: Looks like the rain's stopped for a minute.

BUBBA: Dammit. I'm sorry.

D'LADY: I should go before it starts again—

BUBBA: Shit I thought I fixed this thing.

D'LADY: So, thanks for the shirt—

BUBBA: This isn't supposed to happen.

D'LADY: See you later!

(D'LADY *rushes out the door stopping long enough to give* BUBBA *a kiss on the cheek. He tries for more and misses. The bells stop.*)

BUBBA: Perfect. Pay attention. I didn't need to be reminded.

(BUBBA *stands holding the wires amidst his papers that have been scattered during his struggle with the system.*)

(*Lights fade to black.*)

5.

(*Sun rises to full brightness.* GLORIA *comes out onto her porch with a basket of laundry on her hip. She puts it down beside her and lights a cigarette.*)

GLORIA: Betsy! Betsy! Girl, where are you? Betsy!

BETSY: (*Comes out onto the porch*) I'm here. Here. Here.

GLORIA: Need me to pick anything up for dinner tonight?

BETSY: Yeah…I'm going to make tuna casserole? I just need some celery, maybe an onion?

GLORIA: Think you could make something else?

BETSY: Um…maybe? I don't know. Like what?

GLORIA: It's fine. I'll pick it up after I get this on the line. I need to get some pantyhose anyways. I'm going out later.

BETSY: Is there a party tonight?

GLORIA: Yes. You shouldn't go. Not because you weren't invited, you were—word travels fast around here, but you've got a delicate situation—and I don't think you've got the right outfit.

BETSY: I do.

GLORIA: No, I looked at your things, trust me. You shouldn't go out there yet.

BETSY: But Gloria—

GLORIA: Honey look, there's nothing you can do. This won't always be the case, which is partly why right now I can say this to you. But right now you are helpless. You are orphaned. Now listen—I know what I'm talking about here. Come here.

(GLORIA *holds* BETSY *at arms length.*)

GLORIA: You have never known the security of another's arms so you are grasping and nervous and so no one trusts you—you're better off staying home. The only thing you'll find out there tonight is pity. I don't pity you—and I think you should be spared the false comfort of others.

BETSY: Gloria?

GLORIA: Yes Betsy?

BETSY: You're right not to pity me.

GLORIA: I know. Now go.

BETSY: And thanks for taking me in.

GLORIA: That's enough now.

(GLORIA *kisses* BETSY *on top of her head.* BETSY *exits and* GLORIA *starts hanging laundry on the line.*)

(A dog howls and D'LADY *walks in from the back.)*

*(*D'LADY *stretches her arms wide, yawns. Sees* GLORIA *and* BETSY, *watches them a moment before approaching.)*

D'LADY: Gloria.

GLORIA: Well, here you are. I heard you were in town.

D'LADY: Yeah. Thought it was about time for a visit.

GLORIA: Huh—well, here I am. Been a long time.

D'LADY: You all still here—feels like I never left.

GLORIA: Huh. Mind handing me that sheet?

*(*D'LADY *pulls a damp sheet from the basket.)*

D'LADY: Sure.

GLORIA: Hold it here.

D'LADY: Got it. Who's that girl I saw scurrying back in your house?

GLORIA: Betsy. She turned up at the café looking like a stray cat a couple of weeks ago.

D'LADY: She looks like—where'd she come from?

GLORIA: West somewhere—Colorado—

D'LADY: She's looking for Jimmy isn't she?

GLORIA: I don't ask. I'm giving her a place to stay, she helps me out—I don't snoop around.

D'LADY: Has she seen him?

GLORIA: D'lady—did you just hear me? I leave her be. She'll need more help than I can give soon enough— and hopefully by then she'll be settled enough to take care of herself.

D'LADY: Okay.

GLORIA: Anyways, company's nice.

D'LADY: I guess. Jimmy's back here then?

GLORIA: You just stop by to get the news? Why don't you go around there yourself—he's living with Bubba.

D'LADY: I was over there last night. He didn't mention Jimmy—Is he okay?

GLORIA: Jimmy?

D'LADY: No. Bubba.

GLORIA: He doesn't leave his house.

D'LADY: That doesn't sound good.

GLORIA: He says he's busy with his research. I bring his groceries by, things from the café—Jimmy's helping out now. That's good. Long as he sticks around.

D'LADY: Nobody told me.

GLORIA: How exactly were we supposed to do that?

D'LADY: Call? Write?

GLORIA: At what number? What address? I wasted enough time trying to reach you when my mom was sick. Left messages with all sorts of random strangers—had to tell them my business—explain who I was—you were never there—you never called back—you know how pathetic I felt?

D'LADY: I—I moved a lot—and—I'm sorry—

GLORIA: For what?

D'LADY: About your mom.

GLORIA: I thought you meant that you didn't call.

D'LADY: Gloria—I was gone—I'm sorry—I wasn't thinking.

GLORIA: But you knew.

D'LADY: I didn't know what to say. I couldn't have changed anything.

GLORIA: I didn't need anything changed.

D'LADY: Course not. I'm sorry—I should've called.

GLORIA: She liked you.

D'LADY: I know. I liked her too. And I'm here now—

GLORIA: It was hard. She was sick awhile. When—well after, Jimmy came back for the funeral—and Amory's been a big help.

D'LADY: Bubba's sister?

GLORIA: Married Roy a few years ago. You hear that?

D'LADY: No. I didn't get a lot of news.

GLORIA: Well. What could you have said anyways?

D'LADY: Gloria—

GLORIA: Look—this is a surprise—seeing you. I need to get ready for work. You can come by later—after the lunch crowd if you want.

D'LADY: Like two?

GLORIA: That'd be okay.

(JIMMY *enters in silhouette behind a sheet hanging on the line. He's carrying some heavy bags.* D'LADY'*s attention goes to him.*)

D'LADY: I'll try to stop by.

GLORIA: Don't put yourself out or anything. (*She exits into the house.*)

D'LADY: Jimmy! Jimmy! Remember me? Jimmy! Remember! It's me—D'Lady—Mary—Alice—Jimmy! Hey—over here. It's been awhile—Hey! Jimmy— Jimmy O'Connel you dumbass look at me!

(D'LADY *goes behind the washing to look for him.* JIMMY *comes all the way down stage.*)

JIMMY: In Colorado it looked like this.

(*The sky turns into a flaming sunset.* D'LADY *starts walking forward.*)

JIMMY: D'Lady! D'Lady! Where are you going? Look at me—look at me—D'Lady—Mary Alice! You Bitch! Come on, don't do this—Don't leave me here. D'lady where are you going—can't you hear me?—the middle of fuckin' nowhere. You can't leave me! That's my car! D'Lady.
Come back.
Please.

(Sunset fades. There are stars, a moon, it is the middle of nowhere.)

D'LADY: This is what happened. Nobody cares now, but this is what happened: We drove ten hours west. Parked the car and slept. Tucked up close as orphans with nothing but each other, it's a picture, a poem. When we slept, wrapped up in that blanket, I dreamt of a girl so small he could wrap her up and strap her on his back. He could wrap his long arms around her and love her and stroke her hair. And one night I'm walking outside of town, out to where the melons grow and there was a trailer with a light on and a girl came to the window so slight she was transparent, I could see her cooking her dinner, and I knew. I folded the blanket and put it on the step for her and for him and I left him there. And I went west. *(She exits.)*

JIMMY: I'm in love with a girl in a melon patch. Still I get a letter and off I go.

(BETSY appears.)

BETSY: You were only going to be gone a week.

JIMMY: It was different when I landed.

BETSY: Did you think of me?

JIMMY: On the road I did. Doubled over the steering wheel. I was sick to leave you, kept going with a belly aching full of coffee. Then I was home. I didn't need to think.

BETSY: I worked. I taught myself stuff out there. I don't need you to live. I know that now. So now I know I want you with me.

JIMMY: I got a job.

BETSY: I know

JIMMY: I live with Bubba.

BETSY: Gloria told me.

JIMMY: You live with Gloria. She's a good person.

BETSY: I want you.

JIMMY: My car broke when I got here. I have to walk everywhere.

BETSY: There are few things that I want.

JIMMY: Now my sneakers are wearing down, the soles straight through to my socks. Bubba's mom can get me a discount on some new ones I think.

BETSY: Before you I wanted nothing.

JIMMY: Were you mad when I left?

BETSY: No. When my head cleared and I washed the sheets and I looked at the stars and I knew I'd see you again.

JIMMY: You are not so close to me now.

BETSY: No. I'll get there.

JIMMY: I don't have a chance do I?

BETSY: Chance?

JIMMY: A choice?

BETSY: No.

JIMMY: Sure. Sure—shit.

BETSY: Not then—not now.

JIMMY: Betsy. I kept thinking you were here. Like, you were coming over—walking up to the door—or—I'd

see you, think it was you—in a bus window, or
Once—I thought I saw you playing basketball—

BETSY: I was coming.

JIMMY: Did you know?

BETSY: What's there to know?

(BETSY *kisses* JIMMY.)

JIMMY: Betsy, would you meet me tonight? After work?
I get off at six, and could use a lift home.

BETSY: I don't have a car—or a license. Sure, okay, I'll
be there.

JIMMY: I'll see you then? At six.

BETSY: Wait. Where do you work?

JIMMY: The plant.

BETSY: Right. Six.

JIMMY: Six. *(He exits.)*

BETSY: GLORIA! GLORIA!

GLORIA: Jeezminetly darlin' quiet down. I'm right here.

BETSY: Gloria. I need your car. Tonight. I'm going to
pick him up from work.

GLORIA: You're making dinner tonight. He's going to a
party.

BETSY: I'll make it up, it'll be in the icebox for you. Now
let me have the car.

GLORIA: Look at you. Here it is and there you go.
You're not thinking of me are you? You're not at all,
neither of you, you're all night-time swooning and I'm
just day-time drudgery.

BETSY: Gloria, please I'm thinking of you. I am. I just
need the car, now.

GLORIA: Stop. It's not for you. Look at you, you little thing, you're not ready for it. *(She exits.)*

BETSY: Nothing is for me. Yet me, I will find everything.

(BETSY holds her breath and shuts her eyes tight. The car keys drop from the sky.)

BETSY: Thank you. *(She takes the keys and runs off.)*

6.

(Late Evening. ROY sits the edge of the couch with his head in his hands. AMORY is partially undressed they have just tried to make love.)

AMORY: Roy, there are ten thousand babies at any given moment who need a home.

ROY: Really, ten thousand? Round the world, across the street, where?

AMORY: In the world, in general, the entire world. Orphanages in Eastern Europe for example are full of children. Brimming with babies. And right here there are several agencies who assign families to young women who find themselves pregnant and without the desire or ability to care for the child, or often even themselves, and the family helps the poor girl through her time and then they get the baby—right then—they are part of the whole experience.

ROY: Except conception.

AMORY: No, not conception.

ROY: I want to do this.

AMORY: I know you do.

ROY: And you know I've not had trouble before.

AMORY: No trouble until now.

ROY: And the thing is I don't want you to think its cause I don't want this.

AMORY: I don't think that, I don't think that at all. In fact I think the opposite, that you want it so much it's getting in the way.

ROY: Maybe so.

AMORY: Don't worry, it'll work itself out. *(Kisses him)* Did you ask Bubba about your ghost?

ROY: Not yet—is he okay?

AMORY: As much as anyone.

ROY: I tried to see him after work, he seemed preoccupied.

AMORY: He's devoted to whatever it is he's studying—but there's no form to his research, no direction. What else did you do?

ROY: Work. Had dinner at The Cracker Shack. A cheeseburger and fries.

AMORY: Really? A burger? Have you lost your mind? Do you know what's in that meat? Mad cow disease. You know Alzheimer's doesn't exist in populations who don't consume mass quantities of genetically engineered beef products? Non-industrialized populations do not suffer from these diseases—nor do they suffer from most allergies or pain in childbirth.

ROY: Amory?

AMORY: We have come so far and gained a life plagued by bodies rebelling against the very civilization they exist in. Did you consider this? The rainforests? The cowshit pollution?

ROY: No. I was thinking of that ghost. I needed to be some place noisy.

AMORY: Roy. This has got to stop.

ROY: I know.

AMORY: I think you're tangled up in your feelings about your past and your future and this is intruding on your present.

ROY: I am not tangled up about anything. I am here, with you, we are trying to have a baby.

AMORY: Yet you eat cheeseburgers at the Cracker Shack. I wouldn't be surprised if you had taken up smoking. Your ghosts are no mystery—your nerves wind tighter and tighter the longer that she is in town without speaking to you. It's no secret—It's okay too. I trust you see the big picture and I ask you not to drive yourself crazy over it.

ROY: I'm not smoking.

AMORY: Okay. Would you refrain from eating toxic meat?

ROY: I'll come home for every meal, as long as you're here and I don't have to sit in silence.

AMORY: and what, you just need me for the noise—will my typing fingers do—or do you need my endless stream of conversation?

ROY: No—Amory—that's not—

AMORY: What you meant? Figures. You should figure out what it is you do mean—and maybe that'll clear up your impotence problem as well—or is that just a result of pining over girls you couldn't get in high school.

ROY: We went out—sortof—

AMORY: Oh Jesus, well, don't let me stand in your way.

ROY: Amory—

AMORY: We should stop talking now.

ROY: I didn't mean it like—

AMORY: Don't think about it. I'm going to finish this article. Then I'm going to bed, in the study.

ROY: Don't—Amory—

AMORY: We'll talk about it tomorrow. I also made an appointment with a fertility specialist at nine A M. You're free, I checked your schedule, and you'll come with me. Don't waste anything masturbating. They will need whatever you can produce for the tests.

(AMORY *exits.* ROY *sits with his head in his hands.*)

ROY: Accckkkkk. (*He grabs his coat and exits.*)

7.

(BUBBA's *house at night. He sits in his easy chair, surrounded by papers and books. He is painstakingly typing on Amory's old typewriter. His bell system rigged up overhead. He has a single light on.*)

(D'LADY *watches him a moment from outside, then knocks.*)

D'LADY: Bubba?

BUBBA: Argh. D—

(D'LADY *comes in. She's still wearing* BUBBA's *shirt.*)

D'LADY: Thought I'd come over—

BUBBA: That's my shirt.

D'LADY: I like it.

BUBBA: I'm in the middle of something.

(D'LADY *flops down across from* BUBBA. *He regards her warily.*)

D'LADY: Over by the quik-mart there's a light on. Amory's light. She's been waiting up all night for Roy to come home. She doesn't know he's at my house.

Parked outside my door. Waiting for me to come home and here I am with you.

It's stupid, isn't it? Everyone up all night—wandering from place to place—didn't they hear about how if you're lost you're s'posed to stay still till someone finds you?

BUBBA: That what you do?

D'LADY: Hah. Guess not. I'm never still anymore. There's always something. There's roads, and if the day's getting slow—I drive. I guess I'm still when I drive.

BUBBA: I'm still all the time. That's what I do. Just still. Still here.

D'LADY: Still missing me?

BUBBA: No.

D'LADY: Really?

BUBBA: Do you want some juice or something?

D'LADY: Sure. Thanks.

BUBBA: Beer or apple?

D'LADY: Beer please.

BUBBA: Okay. *(He exits to the kitchen.)*

D'LADY: I miss tons of things—it's crazy—for years there's been no weddings in my life. No funerals.

BUBBA: You come back for funerals?

(BUBBA re-enters with two beers. Hands one to D'LADY)

D'LADY: No—

BUBBA: Good. 'Cause I don't think anyone's fixing to die.

D'LADY: That's not what I meant—

BUBBA: Cheers.

D'LADY: Cheers.

(BUBBA *and* D'LADY *toast cans. Drink*)

D'LADY: All these years slipped by and here you are—

BUBBA: You had my name tucked into your dimple.

D'LADY: Yup. Stuck there. I haven't heard any news for years. Things started falling out of my head. And like—I don't know—I just wanted to hear from someone that knew me.

BUBBA: You didn't make any friends out there?

D'LADY: A few—but—it's not the same.

BUBBA: Guess not.

D'LADY: You wouldn't know—you've always had people around you.

BUBBA: You don't know about what I know.

D'LADY: I know you haven't left the house—

BUBBA: And what does that tell you?

D'LADY: That you'd want to see me?

BUBBA: Really? There's no reason you should think that.

D'LADY: I thought you missed me.

BUBBA: Sure. I missed you perched there—somewhere between kissing and flight—never knowing what you'd do next—hell—maybe you'll take off with Jimmy again—no—how about Roy—he's got a car— and he's all excited you're back.

D'LADY: At least someone is.

BUBBA: Your homecoming disappointing to you?

D'LADY: It's not what I imagined.

BUBBA: Very little is.

D'LADY: You ever imagine me coming back?

BUBBA: I figured you would eventually. Figure you'll leave again too. Glo says I don't have to talk to you, she says I need to shut the door against you.

D'LADY: But you didn't.

BUBBA: You didn't knock—you just walked in—

D'LADY: Then throw me out.

ROY: *(From outside)* Bubba?

D'LADY: Is that Roy?

BUBBA: I'll get rid of him.

D'LADY: No—I'll go. Just don't tell him I was here.

(D'LADY downs her beer and slips out the back door. Sets off BUBBA's bells.)

BUBBA: D wait a second—dammit—you don't have to—

ROY: Hey Bubba—you home? There's something I need to talk to you about.

BUBBA: Sorry—Roy, listen it's not a good time.

ROY: I won't be long—what's going on in there?

BUBBA: Nothing—I'm just working on something—

(The bells stop. BUBBA goes to check for D'LADY.)

ROY: *(Comes inside)* I've got to talk to somebody

BUBBA: Talk to Amory.

ROY: I did, she said to ask you—anyways, I think you'll understand. Do you have a smoke?

BUBBA: Nope.

ROY: Oh. Listen—I'm seeing things.

BUBBA: Roy—

ROY: Come on, listen to me, last Tuesday—I started seeing this thing—out of the corner of my eye, a shape—I think its a woman and she's running after something. It might be her head.

BUBBA: Her head?

ROY: Yeah. I thought it was a ghost—so I thought you might know something about that?

BUBBA: There're civil war stories, soldiers and stuff—out Route 208 there're stories about a kid who died out there—people see him chasing a ball into the street—

ROY: Yeah—no. See—I'm walking, by my house, down the road, past the egg lady's farm. She died. Did you know that?

BUBBA: Yeah. Ms Jennings. Her kids are fighting over the land.

ROY: No one tells me anything.

BUBBA: You don't listen.

ROY: So I'm trying to quiet my thoughts, and I see it again. This time it happens slowly. I see some movement, I think—oh, a rabbit or a raccoon, something furry and wild and nice and my eye goes to it, thinking, I'll tell Amory about the animals I saw and my eyes focus on a tree and hanging from the tree is that head—tied up by two long pig tails, its eyes are staring at me and it opens its mouth—and just then I hear a phone ring. My head turns and I look back and nothing's there. Just a voice, saying "Roy?"

BUBBA: Weird.

ROY: I think it's D'lady's voice.

BUBBA: Oh.

ROY: I mean, it's not about her—

BUBBA: You drive to her house to stare at her window.

ROY: You have a bell rigged into the wall to do what? Keep you focused?

BUBBA: So?

ROY: So, I thought you might understand.

BUBBA: I don't.

ROY: You're lying. Fine.

BUBBA: You want a beer?

ROY: No, I better not. Amory wants to have a baby.

BUBBA: She always has.

ROY: Well, now she's doing something about it. I think she's putting aphrodisiacs in my food.

BUBBA: That would explain your sudden fixation on D'Lady.

ROY: No, look it's not like that.

BUBBA: Really?

ROY: No—

BUBBA: Then what're you doing out there?

ROY: I like the drive okay—

BUBBA: I bet. Look she knows you're parked out there.

ROY: She does?

BUBBA: Yeah, she does.

ROY: Did she tell you that? 'Cause she wants to see me later and if that's—

BUBBA: Wait a minute. She's meeting you?

(JIMMY comes in with BETSY, they kiss and peck their way across the room.)

JIMMY: Roy! What a surprise—good to see you.

ROY: Hi—I was just—

JIMMY: Hey—have you met Betsy?

ROY: Oh—no, not yet.

BETSY: Hi. Nice to meet you.

ROY: You too.

(BETSY *and* ROY *shake hands.*)

BETSY: You must be Bubba?

BUBBA: Yeah—you're the one who was calling here?

BETSY: No—I don't use telephones.

BETSY: *(To* BUBBA*)* You've been here a long time haven't you?

BUBBA: A while.

BETSY: I used to be somewhere like that.

JIMMY: You hungry?

BETSY: A little bit.

BUBBA: There's some mac and cheese in the fridge.

(BETSY *and* JIMMY *kiss.*)

JIMMY: Thanks man—maybe later.

BETSY: Nice to meet you both.

(BETSY *and* JIMMY *make-out while exiting up the stairs.*)

ROY: We are the same age as him. We do not neck young girls in the living room. We do not giggle. What happened? Where did that go for us?

BUBBA: Roy, we never did. Nothing's changed.

ROY: Huh. I better go.

BUBBA: Meeting D'lady—

ROY: No. Yes—I don't know—

BUBBA: Watch out for ghosts.

ROY: Very funny.

BUBBA: I'm serious. You never know what you're looking at.

ROY: Right. 'Night.

(ROY *exits. Lights fade on* BUBBA *opening another beer.*)

8.

(The edge of an old dock)

(Lights rise on D'LADY *opening a beer. There's a six-pack next to her. She smokes a cigarette. The moon is out and shining. There are crickets chirping.)*

*(*ROY *enters. He's awkward, it takes him a while to sit down.)*

D'LADY: Didn't think you were coming.

ROY: Well. Yeah—I haven't been out here in a while.

D'LADY: Really? I'd be out here all the time I think. Want a beer?

ROY: Sure thanks. *(Takes one. Opens it. Sips)* Thanks.

D'LADY: Cheers.

ROY: Cheers. I didn't know what to think when you called. How are you? Are you okay? It must be something coming back—after so long. And I know Bubba's been a mess. Have you seen him? Of course you have. That's a guy who can carry a torch.

D'LADY: Yeah.

ROY: So—how are you? I heard you were living out west?

D'LADY: My mom tell you that?

ROY: It's just what I heard.

D'LADY: I heard you got married.

ROY: Yeah, a couple years ago. Hey, could I get a cigarette from you?

D'LADY: Sure.

ROY: Thanks—I don't usually smoke you know, but— Hey, it's been a long time—hasn't it?

D'LADY: Not so long though—I mean, I saw you last night.

ROY: Oh—

D'LADY: I was curious if you talk to Amory about stuff like that.

ROY: Well, we're having kind of a tough time at the moment. We're going to start counseling next week.

D'LADY: Really?

ROY: It's nothing, just—adjusting to coupledom—you know.

D'LADY: No, I don't know. You should just figure out what it is you mean and say it.

ROY: That's my problem I guess.

D'LADY: What's that?

ROY: Figuring out what it is I mean.

D'LADY: Oh. I heard it was cause you were temporarily impotent.

ROY: What? Where'd you hear that?

D'LADY: Just around.

ROY: Don't people have better things to talk about?

D'LADY: No. Not really. You were parked outside my house last night.

ROY: I like to drive out there. I'm supposed to do things that relax me. That's relaxing.

D'LADY: Oh.

ROY: Sorry—I saw your light on, I thought about ringing the bell—but it was late. So I just sat a minute.

D'LADY: Did it work?

ROY: Look,

D'LADY: Did it? Just remembering? Or did you watch me undress. I knew you were there. I knew it. That's why it took me so long to get out of my clothes—no sense wasting a good memory—there's so few of them.

ROY: D'Lady—

D'LADY: It's kindof sexy isn't it?

ROY: I didn't mean for you to see me.

D'LADY: I meant for you to see me though.

ROY: Huh.

D'LADY: Remember? That day you met me here—right here, hah! I didn't know you had it in you.

ROY: I remember.

D'LADY: It was sweet.

ROY: I felt awful.

D'LADY: For what?

ROY: For Bubba mostly—and for me—I put it out of my mind—until—

D'LADY: Until you felt me coming home.

ROY: Maybe. It's not you though.

D'LADY: Well thanks—

ROY: No—it's—something else—maybe ghosts—or I don't know. There are things we don't understand.

D'LADY: And some we do. Shut your eyes.

ROY: Look. I'm married. I'm having some problems, and my wife and I are working on them.

D'LADY: Relax. I'm not going to touch you. Just shut your eyes.

ROY: What are you going to do?

D'LADY: I'm going to tell you what I think. A place holds onto its favorites. And if you're away and some place wants you it's always dreaming to you and drawing you back. But when you listen and you get yourself where you belong everything works out, you get clear-headed mornings.

ROY: *(Opening his eyes)* Sounds good.

D'LADY: Sure, sounds good, but—turns out it's not that way. Turns out it's all shit. This time it's like the place wants me and is twisting everything around to keep me—but you all don't. You all want me out.

ROY: That's not how it is.

D'LADY: No?

ROY: It's great to see you, okay. Really. But I shouldn't be here. I need to get home.

D'LADY: Home? We are all orphans. We are old orphans and too old to be taken home. Thankfully we're so stupidly hopeful we will call anything home, safe, base.

ROY: *(To himself)* Olly olly oxen free.

D'LADY: Hah! Pucker up.

ROY: What?

D'LADY: Pucker up I said. I am going to kiss you. I want that hopeful tongue of yours in my mouth. I want to taste the hope on your fat tongue.

(D'LADY kisses ROY. He is perplexed.)

ROY: You should go back where you were.

D'LADY: I don't know where I was.

ROY: You shouldn't be here.

D'LADY: In town? Or kissing you?

ROY: Here. With me. I'm sorry about watching you and all. It won't happen again. You should go.

D'LADY: I'm staying here. I will stay here until the moon turns yellow and the fireflies stop blinking.

ROY: So you'll go soon.

D'LADY: Sure soon, look up. The stars are bright here. It's so calm—I never feel like this. Still.

ROY: Amory's waiting for me.

D'LADY: Fine. Go.

ROY: You really shouldn't be out here by yourself.

D'LADY: You worried about me?

ROY: There's strange stuff out here.

D'LADY: I don't think anybody's worried for me for a long time.

ROY: Just be careful.

D'LADY: I'm not afraid of ghosts.

ROY: You've never seen one then.

(ROY *leaves.* D'LADY *sits, lights a cigarette.*)

(*Black out*)

9.

(AMORY *sits on* GLORIA's *porch. Late morning sun drenches the stage.* GLORIA *enters from the house with cups of tea.*)

AMORY: They told me this morning, at the clinic. I don't know—I didn't know what to do—I'd do anything you know? But there's nothing to be done. I can't. It turns out after all I can't have a baby. It just is this way.

GLORIA: I'm sorry.

AMORY: Thanks. I don't understand. I planned for this Gloria—I did, I worked hard. Built this life, for this—we would love, provide, cherish—we would give everything and we get nothing.

GLORIA: Oh, honey, just because it's not how you planned doesn't mean it won't be...

AMORY: I shouldn't be surprised. Statistically I mean. The chemicals we are exposed to in our daily lives—its amazing babies still try to come into this world.

GLORIA: Still.

AMORY: And when they do come, they come to those who don't expect it. Girls too wrapped up in themselves to love a baby.

GLORIA: Like Betsy.

AMORY: She's pregnant?

GLORIA: I think so. She acts like nothing's happening. Like she's invisible. She and D'lady. Drifty women.

AMORY: D'Lady's rootless. You can see it when you look at her. She may feel things—but she doesn't know anything. She's prone to dramatics with a gratuitously romantic imagination.

GLORIA: Maybe but—

AMORY: How long do you think she's been pregnant?

GLORIA: Betsy? I don't know. Not long.

AMORY: It's funny isn't it, the way you get what you don't want and what you want you don't get.

(D'LADY *enters. Invites herself up onto the porch*)

D'LADY: Hi ladies. Sure is beautiful out this morning. You two looked so nice sitting here I thought I'd stop in.

AMORY: Excuse me, I'm—just going to get some more tea. Gloria?

GLORIA: I'm fine.

(AMORY *exits into the house.*)

D'LADY: Is she mad at me?

GLORIA: D'lady—now isn't really the best time—

D'LADY: I just—wanted to say hello. See you—just talk?

GLORIA: She got some difficult news this morning— things don't just stop because you're here.

D'LADY: I know that—maybe I could help?

GLORIA: No. It's serious. D'lady I think you should leave.

D'LADY: Gloria—

(AMORY *re-enters.*)

AMORY: You're still here?

D'LADY: Amory, you don't need to worry.

AMORY: Excuse me?

D'LADY: Just, if you were worried about Roy—

AMORY: I don't expect you to understand anything about a relationship so I'll politely tell you, no. I am not worried about Roy.

D'LADY: Okay, well, good then. Sorry to bother you. (*She exits lighting a cigarette as she goes.*)

GLORIA: It's just not a good time.

D'LADY: Don't worry about it. (*She exits.*)

AMORY: Don't make excuses.

GLORIA: I'm not. It's just, it's strange having her here.

AMORY: You need to set boundaries. Otherwise she'll be dropping by whenever she wants.

GLORIA: I don't mind so much really. Wonder what she'll do?

AMORY: Leave soon hopefully. Her poor mother. Tell me about Betsy.

GLORIA: Betsy? I don't think she grasps that she's pregnant, that she's capable.

AMORY: Women underestimate themselves.

GLORIA: Jimmy's the father.

AMORY: And he's a dud. He'll take off—leave her stranded somewhere—

GLORIA: Love can change people.

AMORY: Not him—I mean maybe at the beginning, but he's no one she and a baby could rely on. A baby needs someone to rely on—a steady home.

GLORIA: Sure but—people make their decisions—things fall into some sort of shape.

AMORY: Have you found that to be the case?

GLORIA: Eventually they do.

AMORY: You could change this. Talk to Betsy. She will listen to you.

GLORIA: She's not listening to anyone but him.

AMORY: Talk to him then. He'll listen to you.

GLORIA: He used to—

AMORY: They're going to have a hard time with this—but we can help. They'll be grateful—Roy and I will take care of everything—

GLORIA: You and Roy?

AMORY: We can provide a home. That's all anyone needs isn't it? A real home? Can I use your phone?

GLORIA: Sure.

(AMORY *exits inside.* GLORIA *picks up her mug and follows her in.*)

10.

(BUBBA's house. *He's working on his device, he's dismantled it and parts and wires are laid out.*)

(JIMMY *is pacing back and forth.*)

JIMMY: Look man, I don't know what you should do. Depends what she's up to. And she probably doesn't even know what that is.

BUBBA: She keeps coming over.

JIMMY: Don't let her in.

BUBBA: She just comes.

JIMMY: Then you leave.

BUBBA: Dude.

JIMMY: Hell I don't know. Thing is though you gotta do something. I've been back since the end of May and you've done nothing—

BUBBA: I am doing something.

JIMMY: Dude—really? You're not. C'mon—

BUBBA: I've been reading. Putting together these scraps of things nobody's done this before—these are people's lives—

JIMMY: What about yours?

BUBBA: What about it?

JIMMY: She's back for you. You know that don't you?

BUBBA: She's not.

JIMMY: She is. She never stopped talking about you. Hell—I think she thought you'd steal a car and come after her. Show up one night, punch me in the face and carry her off into the sunset.

BUBBA: What were you thinking?

JIMMY: I don't know—Dude, I wasn't thinking. D'lady was talking in my ear a mile a minute talking about all the things we'd find out there. Pretty quick it was clear she was hung up on you. We were broke most of the time—stuck with each other.

BUBBA: You found Betsy out there.

JIMMY: I didn't find her. D'Lady did.

(D'LADY *knocks on* BUBBA's *door.*)

JIMMY: And here she is.

D'LADY: *(Entering)* Bubba? Oh—hi—Jimmy—

JIMMY: Good—bye D'lady.

D'LADY: You don't have to—

JIMMY: Yeah I do. *(He acknowledges* BUBBA *and exits.)*

D'LADY: Jesus. I can't go anywhere.

BUBBA: It'll get better.

D'LADY: No. Not really. I don't think it will. I know everything here. I know the turns—the streets, the homes—and I'm lost.

BUBBA: C'mon.

D'LADY: What? Nobody wants to talk to me.

BUBBA: That's not true.

D'LADY: Are you even glad to see me?

BUBBA: Sure.

D'LADY: Jimmy's not. He can't get away from me fast enough.

BUBBA: D'lady that's not it—

D'LADY: Amory's not. Gloria's not. Nobody really—my mom keeps asking me what I'm doing, if I'm staying long.

BUBBA: D'lady, we're all glad to see you.

D'LADY: No you're not. You don't know what to do with me. It'd be fine if I was visiting or something, but if I'm staying then you don't know.

BUBBA: You're staying?

D'LADY: I don't know. Look. My mom told me. Bubba hasn't moved. Bubba's lost his job—and I'd think, he misses me. Bubba. He loves me. Maybe he loves me. But he's not calling, he's not sending letters, why isn't he calling? Why isn't he sending letters? Is he okay?

BUBBA: I'm fine.

D'LADY: No you're not. Sorry but, actually you're not.

BUBBA: Actually it's none of your business.

D'LADY: No?

BUBBA: No.

D'LADY: I missed you.

BUBBA: Really? That why you're back?

D'LADY: Maybe—partly—

BUBBA: Well I heard you didn't get it together. That you'd run off with a painter. That you'd gotten pregnant, had an abortion. I heard you nearly ran Jimmy over with your car. You'd gotten arrested for D W I. That you were being stalked by some asshole. I heard plenty and nothing from you—nothing about you missing me.

D'LADY: Guess there's a lot of talk out there.

BUBBA: Guess so.

D'LADY: For two people who aren't doing anything sure is a lot of talk out there.

BUBBA: Guess so.

Pause

BUBBA: I was in the middle of something here.

D'LADY: Can I watch?

BUBBA: Don't you have something better to do?

D'LADY: No.

BUBBA: Fine. Don't touch anything.

11.

(GLORIA *sits on her porch. The sun is setting.* BETSY *comes up, shaking and slightly delirious, her clothes in disarray, her hair disheveled.*)

BETSY: Gloria, I don't feel well.

GLORIA: I should say so, you don't look well either—

BETSY: I can't sleep.

GLORIA: You're out all night—

BETSY: I can't eat.

GLORIA: Chasin' that boy around.

BETSY: I want him.

GLORIA: I know.

BETSY: I don't know what to do. I'm—

GLORIA: Going to have a baby.

BETSY: You know?

GLORIA: Yes. Honey, I know—I thought so. Look at you—

BETSY: I kept tellin' myself I wasn't—I couldn't—How could I? There's not one soft place on my body. I'm like a spear of asparagus. I'm nothing. How can I be—

GLORIA: The way it always happens—

BETSY: But how am I going to do this? I can't do this. I don't have a safe place to put myself—how am I going find a safe place for a baby?

GLORIA: Jimmy?

BETSY: You think?

GLORIA: What do you think?

BETSY: I don't know—maybe? Maybe he could and if—
if he would then I could—we could make a home—

GLORIA: What if he can't?

BETSY: Why can't he?

GLORIA: Won't? Doesn't? Does and then disappears?
What if you're left? But not just you—you and this
little one? This little baby? How would you?

BETSY: I don't know.

GLORIA: Come here.

BETSY: I don't know.

GLORIA: I know. Okay? I can help. You see? Let me
help.

BETSY: But Jimmy—

GLORIA: I don't know. He already left you once—he
does that—just disappears. If you want, I'll help. We'll
find a place for the baby, I know of one.

BETSY: Babies need homes.

GLORIA: She'll have one, a real home and it will be
fine—

BETSY: Gloria?

GLORIA: Yes?

BETSY: Pity me now?

GLORIA: Yes, go on in to sleep.

(GLORIA *helps* BETSY *inside. Lights fade on* GLORIA's
porch.)

(*Lights up on* ROY *and* AMORY *in their living room.*)

ROY: I don't know.

AMORY: What do you mean you don't know?

ROY: It's not the same is it?

AMORY: Well—no, it's not the same.

ROY: What if we can't love it?

AMORY: We will.

ROY: It won't be my own—

AMORY: He or she will be ours

ROY: And you?

AMORY: Roy—I have no choice.

ROY: You know?

AMORY: I know. There's nothing going to change here.

ROY: This isn't what we planned when we fell in love.

AMORY: I know—

ROY: Can we name it ourselves?

AMORY: We can, of course we can, she's going to move in so we'll watch her grow—swell up—we'll feed her and take care of her and our baby will get bigger inside her—

ROY: Betsy.

AMORY: What about her?

ROY: What will happen to Betsy, after?

AMORY: She'll go home.

ROY: Home?

AMORY: To Gloria's—maybe she'll move though, she'll probably move.

ROY: Amory, do you really think?

AMORY: Yes, I do.

ROY: She's young.

AMORY: Not that young.

ROY: Still—she's just starting out—she probably doesn't know what she wants.

AMORY: Which is exactly why this is for the best—for her, for us, for the baby—

ROY: Did you know what you wanted then?

AMORY: When?

ROY: Before—before we got married?

AMORY: Yes.

ROY: I think that's rare.

AMORY: I considered the options. I think I made very good choices.

ROY: I don't know if I ever knew—if I ever considered—

AMORY: Roy. There's a lot to be done.

ROY: Let's not do anything.

AMORY: And what?

ROY: And nothing—she's young—anything can happen—

AMORY: Things do not just happen. I think you would have noticed that in our lives things have not just happened. Instead I have worked—we have worked and that's why we have a home and—

ROY: Some things just happen.

AMORY: Sure—but we have to make the best choices with what we have. She has a baby she can't care for and we can—that's what we have.

ROY: D'lady kissed me— *(Pause)* and I stopped seeing the ghosts.

AMORY: She—

ROY: I didn't ask her to, she just did.

AMORY: And you let her?

ROY: I didn't do anything. I just stood there—it just happened.

AMORY: It doesn't work like that Roy.

ROY: How does it work then? Cause I can't control everything.

AMORY: No. You can't. Would you please stay at Bubba's tonight?

ROY: Amory.

AMORY: I don't want to talk to you. Please. Go to my brother's house.

ROY: I just—I wanted to tell you—

AMORY: I don't care. Go. Just go.

ROY: No, I want you to talk to me about this—

AMORY: Stop. Please. Just let this happen.

ROY: We'll talk tomorrow.

AMORY: Okay. Go.

ROY: Alright. Maybe that's best right now. I'll stay there tonight—I'll call you in the morning.

AMORY: Go.

ROY: Okay.

(ROY *exits.* AMORY *is left alone. She sits very still.*)

12.

(*Lights up on* GLORIA's *porch. She's looking for something to wish on.* JIMMY *comes rushing up her walk.*)

JIMMY: Gloria. Hi. Is Betsy here?

GLORIA: She's asleep. Don't wake her.

JIMMY: She was supposed to come over but I went out—

GLORIA: She needs to sleep. Really needs it—and you, you don't let her sleep. You give her no peace.

JIMMY: She ain't lookin' for peace.

GLORIA: What do you think she's looking for? You?

JIMMY: I don't know. Maybe. Thanks for letting her crash with you.

GLORIA: She needed someone to look after her. She doesn't have any family.

JIMMY: I know.

GLORIA: She needs a home. Especially now.

JIMMY: She can't stay with you?

GLORIA: She can—but—Jimmy, she's going to have a baby.

JIMMY: A baby?

GLORIA: In about six months.

JIMMY: Mine?

GLORIA: Hers. But—a baby needs a home.

JIMMY: Of course. Damn—I don't know—

GLORIA: Well, she could stay here and when she has it we'll find a good safe home, a peaceful place, regular and full of love.

JIMMY: She agreed to this? I've got to talk to her

GLORIA: No—let her rest now.

JIMMY: Gloria, come on, let me in.

GLORIA: No Jimmy. Go home. Bubba is waiting for you.

JIMMY: Let him wait—come on, she's pregnant and you're trying to tell me what's going to happen with my baby—

GLORIA: No Jimmy—now you listen. I've known you what—sixteen years? Longer? I know how things fall out of your head—you've never loved anyone, you've never made that stuff work—Anna, Cynthia— disappearing with D'lady—you'd just forget to call— hell—me? you remember that one?

JIMMY: Glo of course, but—

GLORIA: You had that dog—you lost it. Do you think suddenly—bang there's a baby so it'll all work out?

JIMMY: I don't know. I've never been in love. I am now.

GLORIA: You are? How do you know?

JIMMY: Look at me for Christsakes—I've never looked like this before—never. You should know that. You of all people should know that.

GLORIA: You look desperate. That's not love. You've not given anything up. Not a damn thing. Selfish is what you are. Go home.

JIMMY: No, I know how I feel about this now.

GLORIA: And I think you're wrong.

JIMMY: She doesn't want to see me?

GLORIA: No. She doesn't. You don't make anything easier for her. She needs real help.

JIMMY: I've got a job.

GLORIA: Okay.

JIMMY: I've got a bike. A room at Bubba's, two pairs of pants, a pair of shoes I've been trying to replace for a year, a haircut I've been planning on getting for a couple of months—

GLORIA: Jimmy I know.

JIMMY: Seven pairs of boxers and seven white t-shirts. Dammit.

GLORIA: Honey, it won't always be like this.

JIMMY: No? I've got nothing Gloria. I've never had anything. What am I thinking? You're right. You are. She should give that baby up to someone who can provide for her.

GLORIA: We'll do that honey. It'll be okay. It will. This is for the best.

JIMMY: Is it a girl?

GLORIA: Betsy thinks so.

JIMMY: Betsy.

(BETSY *comes to the window.*)

BETSY: *(From inside)* Jimmy?

JIMMY: Betsy? Baby?

BETSY: Jimmy. Why'd you ever leave me?

JIMMY: I'll never do it again. I'll get us a car. I'll get it. I'll take you out of here—just hold tight baby—

(JIMMY *runs to get a car. All the stars come out.*)

BETSY: Will he?

GLORIA: I don't know. He's never looked like that before. *(She gives* BETSY *a squeeze and exits inside.)*

(BETSY *sits out on the porch.*)

13.

(ROY *stands on* BUBBA's *porch.* D'LADY's *leaning against the door smoking a cigarette.*)

D'LADY: It's late.

ROY: Amory kicked me out.

D'LADY: Huh. So you want to run away with me?

ROY: I thought you were staying?

D'LADY: Why? Cause I'm not gone yet? Clearly I just fuck things up—Amory wants me gone, Bubba's, well—I don't know—Glo's even sick of me and I've only seen her like twice.

ROY: The only reason they're sick of you is they don't know what you're going to do next—whether you're here or not. So—stay if you want to. We'll adjust.

D'LADY: It'd be different.

ROY: Yeah it would—it'd be good. Hell—Amory could use someone other than me to be sick of.

D'LADY: I don't know—stay? Here? Maybe the notion of here's what's stopping me from slipping away out there? You know? Then when I'm here, like the idea of there will take its place? How do you deal with that?

(Headlights cross the stage. The sound of car tires on gravel)

ROY: Shit—get out of here.

D'LADY: What?

ROY: Would you mind disappearing?

D'LADY: You just said—

ROY: Yeah—but I just saw Amory's car pull around the corner. I don't want her to think—

D'LADY: Let her. You said you'd all get used to me—

ROY: I said we would—not that we had—c'mon, please? Go inside.

D'LADY: I can't. Bubba's fed up with me—

ROY: So—he'll get over it. Shoot—damn it. Look casual.

(AMORY enters.)

D'LADY: Want a smoke?

ROY: NO! Jesus put it out.

D'LADY: Why?

AMORY: I can't believe it.

ROY: I just was going inside—she was on the porch.

D'LADY: Hi Amory.

AMORY: Roy—I was coming to talk to you—and apologize for jumping to conclusions and I see that I was wrong to second-guess myself. So I'll leave and let you two get back to your smoking and conversation— or whatever.

ROY: Amory—stop it—please—here—let's talk—

AMORY: I've lost interest in it.

D'LADY: I'll leave.

AMORY: No. You stay. You stay right here as long as you want. We're all so happy to see you—

D'LADY: Look—I didn't mean to mess anything up.

AMORY: Oh. Don't flatter yourself. It's not you—it's what is it honey? Ghosts right? Just creepy things in the night that call your name?

ROY: I can't help it if I see things.

AMORY: No, apparently you can't help it if people kiss you either.

D'LADY: Amory—look—sorry okay? It wasn't his fault, I don't know—I was just trying to make something happen.

AMORY: Well you did.

D'LADY: Sure but—

AMORY: What? You didn't plan out what's next? See that's the part you never really grasped is it? Not when you left my brother cold—or what else you been up to? Just dropping by to see him? Really—you should think about what's next. Here. I'm an expert at this. Decide to leave. Leave. And the consequence will be that we can carry on with our lives as we were. Not bad really.

ROY: Amory, stop it—it's not about her.

AMORY: No? Then what's it about?

ROY: Us. Okay? Just us.

(BETSY *on* GLORIA's *porch*)

BETSY: I looked up, I looked up and all I could see were stars. Blink and there are stars, blink, blank sky and stars. And I look again. Blink and there is Jimmy.

(JIMMY *runs up to* BUBBA's *porch at full tilt, passes everybody on his way to the door.*)

ROY: Jimmy—hey—what's up?

AMORY: Slow down—Jimmy wait—

D'LADY: He can't.

JIMMY: It's time—it's rolling over me, overwhelming me—Betsy. Her name. Betsy—ringing like a bell. If I don't it will haunt me till I'm dead.
I see her across the street—She's at her window, I'm in her mind—I want to be there, beside her hand. I'll hold it. She'll understand.
I hear her breathing my name, under her breath. When she moves I can see her tiny breast. I want to hold her, clutch her tight—Bubba, this is good-bye—

AMORY: You don't have to leave—you can both stay here—we'll help you—

JIMMY: We can't—we, sorry but we've got to get out of town—get a car—just go, you know? Start over?

AMORY: No—how? And a baby coming? You can't— you don't know anything about being a father. Do you? Do you even have insurance?

ROY: Amory—honey—

JIMMY: I don't know—we'll—just—we'll be together.

AMORY: That's not enough! That's not—

D'LADY: Go. Catch.

(D'LADY *tosses* JIMMY *the keys. He catches them.*)

JIMMY: Really?

AMORY: What are you doing? You have no idea about these things—

ROY: Honey—stop it.

(ROY *gets between* AMORY *and* D'LADY, *walks her off the porch. She may resist, but* ROY *physically guides her.*)

D'LADY: Watch the oil light—and the wheel pulls left—

JIMMY: You mean it?

D'LADY: Go—come back to visit.

(JIMMY *goes to embrace* D'LADY, *then runs inside.*)

JIMMY: I'm going Bubba—I'm going to get my things.

BUBBA: Don't take any of my stuff.

JIMMY: I won't—I got what I need. (*He runs upstairs.*)

AMORY: They—what did they do to deserve this? It's not fair, it's not fair.

ROY: Honey—we'll figure something out. Just not that way. Honey. Some other way.

AMORY: What about that baby? How can they take care of a little baby? They don't have anything.

ROY: They have plenty.

AMORY: They don't know—they just don't know—

ROY: Let me take you home.

AMORY: Home, they don't even have a home.

ROY: Amory—it's not that simple—

AMORY: It should be.

ROY: Well, its not—nothing is.

(ROY *kisses* AMORY *and she rests into his arms. They exit together.* BUBBA *comes out to the doorway.*)

BETSY: I look up and all I can see is you. *(She looks up at the sky.)*

BUBBA: You gave him your car.

D'LADY: I owed him.

BUBBA: But, how will you get back—

D'LADY: Get back where? All I have is this place stuck in my head. You know what it's like—to have something stuck in your head?

BUBBA: I don't know anything.

D'LADY: Don't you? You're the one studying this place. Seems like you'd know what's so damn great about it.

BUBBA: You're staying?

D'LADY: What would you put up a plaque for?

BUBBA: You.

D'LADY: Bubba.

BUBBA: It'd say. D'lady Mary Alice lived here sometimes. Or maybe— On this spot D'Lady Mary Alice looked back at Bubba's house one time before jumping into his best friends car and never thinking of him again.

D'LADY: That's not right.

BUBBA: You didn't look back?

D'LADY: I did. I saw you. You just watched me leave. You didn't do anything. I never understood why you watched. Didn't chase me. Didn't shout. Nothing.

BUBBA: I didn't think I could change anything.

D'LADY: You can. Turns out you can.

(BUBBA *looks at* D'LADY *a moment. She moves to kiss him. He meets her halfway.*)

(They kiss.)

(He pulls away, holds her at arms length.)

BUBBA: D—wait—can you wait? Tomorrow maybe.

D'LADY: Tomorrow?

BUBBA: Or the next day—I need to get focused—

D'LADY: Isn't that what your bells are for?

BUBBA: I'm just not ready now. But stay, okay?

D'LADY: I don't have anywhere else to go.

BUBBA: You don't have to go anywhere else—just—

D'LADY: What?

BUBBA: Just give me a minute.

D'LADY: A minute?

BUBBA: Some time.

D'LADY: Okay. Okay—I can do that. What do I do till then?

BUBBA: I don't know—

D'LADY: Can't drive anywhere.

BUBBA: Try walking.

D'LADY: Right. Walk. *(She kisses him again.)*

(D'LADY exits, walks over to GLORIA's house.)

(JIMMY rushes out the door with his bag packed.)

JIMMY: Bubba—man, I'm going to be a father.

BUBBA: Congratulations.

JIMMY: You too man.

BUBBA: For what?

JIMMY: Getting out of the house. There she is—Betsy! *(He goes to her.)*

BETSY: Blink. And all there was, was him.

JIMMY: Betsy—

BETSY: JIMMY!

(BETSY *jumps off the porch into* JIMMY's *arms.*)

JIMMY: So—you want to—

BETSY: Yes. Anywhere.

(JIMMY *carries* BETSY *off. The sound of a car starting up and driving away.*)

(GLORIA *rushes out onto the porch. Stops and just watches them leave.*)

D'LADY: Glo—

GLORIA: That your car?

D'LADY: Was—theirs now.

GLORIA: Huh. You think they'll be okay?

D'LADY: I don't know.

GLORIA: Hope they let us know how it turns out.

D'LADY: Yeah. Me too.

GLORIA: Want a beer or something?

D'LADY: Sure. Thanks.

(GLORIA *exits in the house.* D'LADY *sits down on her porch.*)

(*Lights fade and the night gets brighter.* BUBBA *exits his house—comes out into the world, looks up at the night sky.*)

(GLORIA *comes back out and sits down next to* D'LADY.)

D'LADY: Glad you're home tonight.

GLORIA: What's out there to see anyway?

D'LADY: Plenty.

(*The ladies open their beers and toast each other.*)

BUBBA: There's the sky. Here's this place. And there she is. Back home. And here I am. Home. Back home.

(Sounds of crickets. A shooting star. Cars in the distance)
(Black out)

END OF PLAY

www.ingramcontent.com/pod-product-compliance
Lightning Source LLC
Chambersburg PA
CBHW052221090426
42741CB00010B/2627